God, grant me the serenity to accept

the things I cannot change;

Courage to change the things I can;

and

Wisdom to know the difference.

Commemorating the
50th
Wedding Anniversary of
David and Anna Boschmann

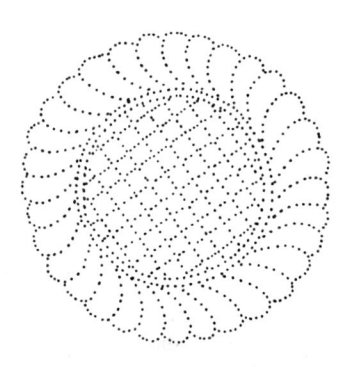

Thoughts To Live By

Erwin Boschmann
Editor

Judy Bauer Boschmann
Art

Published by

SE

SCIENCE ENTERPRISES, INC.
Indianapolis, Indiana

Copyright ©, 1987 by SCIENCE ENTERPRISES, INC.
P. O. Box 88443
Indianapolis, IN 46208

Art Copyright ©, 1987 by Judy Bauer Boschmann

ISBN 0-930116-05-4

Copy editing by Karl C. Illg

All rights reserved. No part of this publication may be reproduced, stored in a retrieval system, or transmited, in any form or by any means, electronic, mechanical, photocopying, recording, or otherwise, without the prior written consent of the publisher.

Printed in the United States of America.

Contents

Preface	7
1. The Creator of Life	9
2. Life Abundant	15
3. Life with our Neighbor	23
4. The Emotions of Life	33
5. The Business of Life	45
6. The Serene Life	63

Preface

We become what we think. And we think what we feed our mind. Gloomy thoughts bring gloomy lives, but good thoughts foster a wholesome life. The well-nourished mind knows no limits.

This book honors the lives of David and Anna Kaethler Boschmann, who celebrated their 50th wedding anniversary on April 10, 1987. To themselves, to their children and grandchildren, and to their community, our parents exemplify the good use of power thoughts.

As children we saw them collect and cherish good quotes, we heard them use quotes in conversation, and in prepared and impromtu speeches. We, too, were encouraged to memorize quotes, verses, and poems. We were encouraged to recite these and, by example, we were encouraged to read and collect worthy thoughts.

As a parent I am pleased to see my children make their own collection of quotes, be they in the form of loose papers, scribbled in school notebooks, or purchased as calendars. I cannot remember a time when our refrigerator door has not had some food for thought attached to it . My children's contributions are often amusing, often challenging, but always a blessing. I vividly remember the day I saw the following new quote on the refrigerator door: "You can tell the size of a man by the size of the thing that makes him mad."

David and Anna continue to read widely, and to collect and study that which is true and good. I have seen Mother, while shopping, pull out a notebook and copy a

"Sinnspruch" (proverb). In her notebook entitled <u>Sinn-sprüche</u> she can quickly mark those that are most important to her. When asked to write down some of his best-liked quotes, Dad was able to sit down and in a matter of hours type out over 70 quotes - complete with rhyme and author reference. Life, indeed, is an ongoing learning experience and we continue to benefit from their learning through their quote-embellished letters.

Why quotes? As Michel de Montaigne said, "I quote others only the better to express myself." Quotes synthesize the essence of human thought and experience. They are the finest distillates of life.

Many delightful insights into human nature are summarized in funny, tongue-in-cheek, syrupy sweet, or even cynical quotes. There are also those sayings which only point out human shortcomings. This book, however, gathers what our families have been fondest of: quotes that are positive, instructive and uplifting; thoughts that encourage self-improvement and call out the very best in human nature.

We hope you benefit from this collection contributed by three generations.

Erwin Boschmann
April 10, 1987

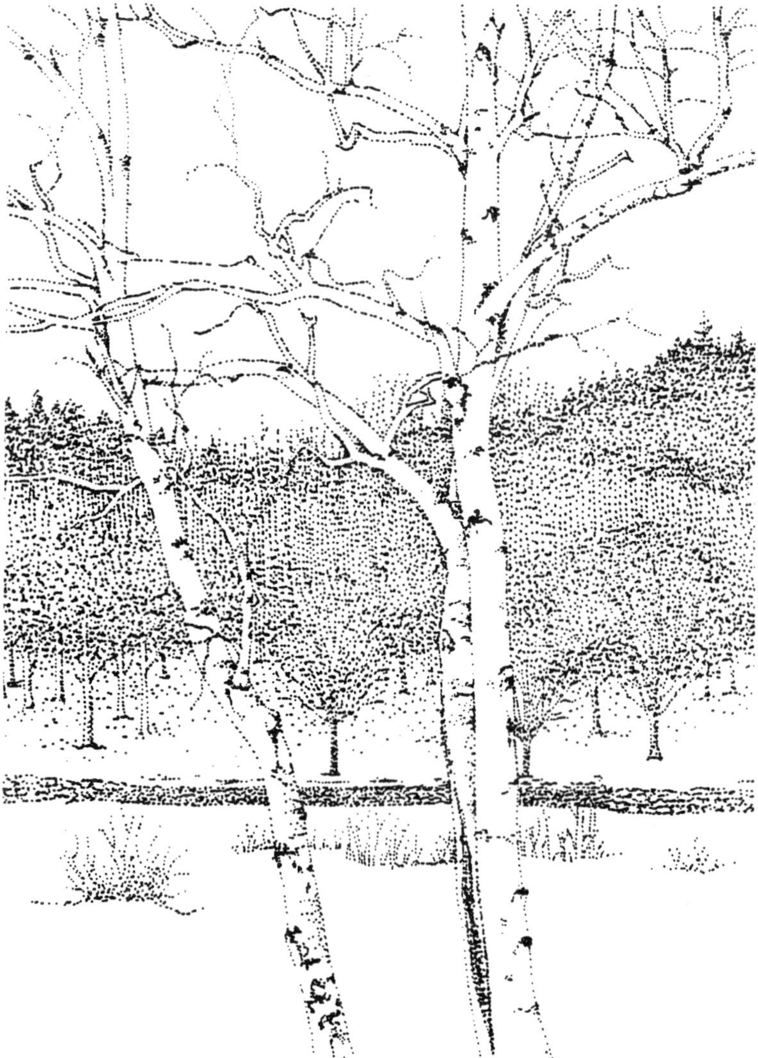

1. The Creator of Life

Faith

Hope

Prayer

The Lord is my shepherd.
-Psalms 23:1

~

God does not love us because we are so worthy,
but we are worthy because he loves us so.
-Helmuth Thieleke

~

Being thankful creates a new face of life.
-Rainer Schmidt

~

God is with us, not only in the light of fulfillment,
but also in the darkness of despair.
-Martin Luther King

~

Earthly hope without an eternal wellspring
becomes but chasing haste.
-F. von Bodelschwing

~

Those who live with hope, see farther;
Those who live with love, see deeper;
Those who live with faith, see everything
in a different light.

~

To feel as God's child brings peace,
to live as one brings joy.

Philosophy seeks truth,
theology finds it,
and religion owns it.

~

Prayer is the service we can do for all mankind.
-Walther Coes

~

Prayer to God about the task at hand
is the heartfelt language of courageous men.

~

God can stand by your side or send an angel to do
what you cannot.
-Christof Blumhard

~

Walk the straight roads, for always they are the shortest;
paths of truth lead securely to the goal.
-Friedrich Hebbel

~

I cannot believe that God plays dice with the universe.
-Albert Einstein

~

God without man is still God;
but man without God is nothing.

I lift up my eyes to the hills-
  where does my help come from?
My help comes from the Lord,
  the Maker of heaven and earth.
He will not let your foot slip-
  he who watches over you will not slumber;
indeed, he who watches over Israel
  will neither slumber nor sleep.
The Lord watches over you-
  the Lord is your shade at your right hand;
the sun will not harm you by day,
  nor the moon by night.
The Lord will keep you from all harm-
  he will watch over your life;
the Lord will watch over your coming and going
  both now and forevermore.
-Psalms 121

~

Miracles are not contrary to nature,
but only contrary to what we know about nature.
-St. Augustine

2. Life Abundant

Children

Body and Mind

Self Discipline

Maturing

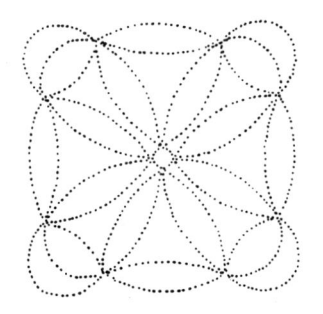

Children

A wise son maketh a glad father.
-Proverbs 10:1

~

Thanks for the sweet things you said about my little boy...
No man can possibly know what life means,
what the world means, what anything means,
until he has a child and loves it.
-Lafcadio Hearn

~

He that will have his son have respect for him
and his orders, must himself have great reverence
for his son.
-John Locke

~

What the father hath hid cometh out in the son;
and oft have I found in the son
the father's revealed secret.
-Friedrich Nietzsche

~

Children are candidly honest, and unashamed of the truth.
-Pasternack in 'Dr. Zhivago'

There are only two lasting bequests we can give our
children: one is roots and the other, wings.

~

Man's most serious activity is play.
                                        -George Santayana

~

If you don't take care of your body,
where are you going to live?

~

Body and Mind

Mens sana in corpore sano.
(Healthy mind in healthy body)

~

Good for the body is the work of the body,
good for the soul is the work of the soul,
and good for either is the work of the other.
                                        -Henry David Thoreau

~

Keep your face in the sunshine,
and you cannot see the shadow.
                                        -Helen Keller

Of all the things you wear,
your expression is the most important.

~

Nature gives you the face you have at twenty;
it is up to you to merit the face you have at fifty.
-Gabrielle "Coco" Chanel

~

What we are is God's gift to us,
what we become is our gift to God.

~

Your outer life is an expression of your inner life.
-Donald Curtis

~

Self Discipline

What you must dare: is to be yourself.
-Dag Hammarskjoeld

~

Don't expect anything original from an echo.

~

What he thinks is what he really is.
-Proverbs 23:7

If you weren't you, would you want to live with yourself-
just as you now are?

~

You grow up the day you have the first real laugh-
at yourself.
-Ethel Barrymore

~

Don't let your thoughts be concerned only with yourself.
-Norman Vincent Peale

~

Have patience with all things,
but first of all with yourself.
-St. Francis de Sales

~

Maturing

The sign of Christmas is a star, a light in darkness.
See it not outside yourself, but shining
in the heaven within.
-A Course in Miracles

~

Remember, no one can make you feel inferior
without your consent.
-Eleanor Roosevelt

The increase in wisdom is measured by the decrease in gall.
-Nietzsche

~

Who has not known misfortune,
can neither seize nor hold fortune.
-David Voit

~

No one is good by chance, that virtue must be learned.
-Seneca

~

I hold the maxim no less applicable to public than to
private affairs: that honesty is always the best policy.
-George Washington

~

Taking fills the hands, giving fills the heart.

~

Learn to discern the real from the false,
the ever-fleeting from the everlasting.
Learn above all to separate head-learning
from soul-wisdom, the 'Eye' from the 'Heart' doctrine.
-H. P. Blavatsky

~

Reaching and holding I've done since birth,
now I'm learning to let go.

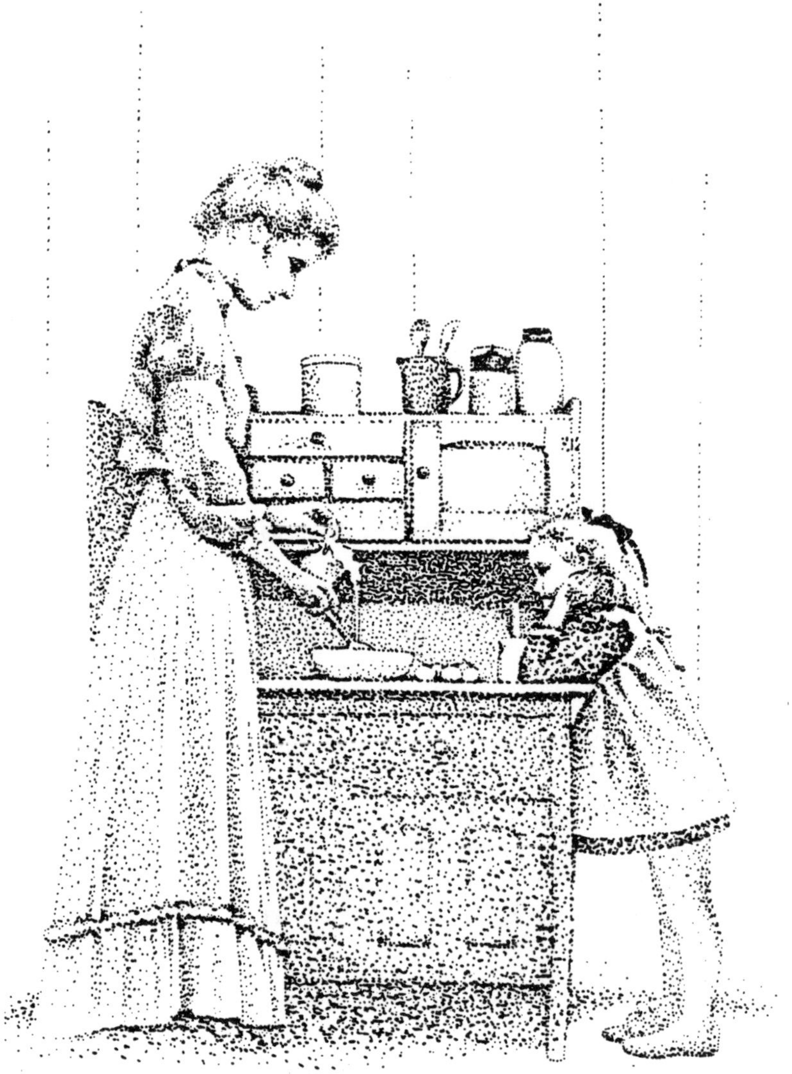

3. Life with our Neighbor

Friendship

Care

Devotion

Friendship

Man cannot think enough of man.
-I. Kant

~

Anyone nearby with a burden is your neighbor.
-Fritz von Bodelschwing

~

The first rule of life is friendliness toward everyone.
-Moltke

~

Be friendly to all, then all will be friendly to you.

~

To know thyself, look at others.
To understand others, look into your heart.
-Schiller

~

The road to the "I" always leads over the "You."

~

Friendship is always a sweet responsibility,
never an opportunity.

It is not lack of love but lack of friendship that makes
unhappy marriages.
          -Friedrich Nietzsche

~

True friendship comes when silence between two
people
is comfortable.
          -Dave Tyson Gentry

~

Peace is not the absence of conflict,
but the ability to cope with it.

~

Teach me to disagree without being disagreeable.
          -Father James Keeler

~

A friend is someone who sticks up for you
when you are not around to defend yourself.

~

A sorrow shared is but half a trouble, but a joy's
shared is a joy made double.

~

Friendship doubles our joys and divides our grief.

Do not quickly break the thread of friendship;
for even if mended, a knot does remain.

~

Care

The wit of conversation lies less in showing it yourself,
than in bringing it out in others.
-B. Franklin

~

To listen well is as powerful a means of influence as to talk
well, and is essential to all true conversation.

~

I have learned silence from the talkative;
tolerance from the intolerant; and
kindness from the unkind.
-Kahlil Gibran

~

Kindness in words creates confidence,
kindness in thinking creates profoundness,
kindness in giving creates Love.
-Lao-tse

~

A friendly word costs nothing, and is the best of all gifts.
-Maurier

True devotion to our neighbor keeps us from premature aging.
-Morton Hemt

~

The best is not clarified with words;
the spirit with which we act is the highest.
-J. W. von Goethe

~

Not what, but how we give determines the value of a gift.
Only true love for our neighbor ennobles our charity.
-Fr. v. Weech

~

No higher joy than to bring joy to others.
-Monier Williams

~

Spread joy, and you will be happy.
-Victor Bluetgen

~

Among all the great and immortal feats: to bring joy to others is the best we can do in this world.
-P. K. Rosegger

~

Helping others is the rent we pay for living on earth.

The greatest joy in life is to ease the burdens for someone.
-Paul Keller

~

If happiness is your goal in life, make others happy;
for the joy that you bestow returns into your own heart.

~

If each would help the other, all would be helped.
-Marie v. Ebner Eschenbach

~

Love and passion may go, but good will is eternal.
-Goethe

~

Devotion

Love and respect cannot be legislated,
they must be earned.
-Zschokke

~

To dry a tear is more honorful
than to sacrifice streams of blood.
-Byron

Seek out man with the heart - not the lantern,
for to love alone does man respond.
-P. Rosegger

~

He who cannot forgive others breaks the bridge
over which he himself must pass.
-Confucius

~

True charity is to bless him who has hurt you.
-Arabic

~

One of the greatest arts of living is the art of forgiving.

~

Don't judge any man until you have walked two moons
in his moccasins.
-Native American Proverb

~

Judge not until you have been in his situation.
-Talmud

~

Judge a man by his questions rather than by his answers.
-Voltaire

I was angry with my friend:
   I told my wrath, my wrath did end.
I was angry with my foe:
   I told it not, my wrath did grow.
-William Blake

~

Your soul is nourished when you are kind,
it is destroyed when you are cruel.
-Proverbs 11:17

~

The tongue extends farther than the hand.

~

God does not want me to mold my neighbor according to a picture of my design.
-D. Bonhoeffer

~

Confront improper conduct, not by retaliation,
but by example.

~

Do unto others as you would have them do unto you.
-Matthew 7:12

4. The Emotions of Life

Love

Challenges

Joy

Happiness

Love

Blessedness is the depth of feeling.

-Schefer

~

There isn't any formula or method.
You learn to love by loving....

-Aldous Huxley

~

To love is to do the noblest of things;
without love life is folly.

-Dschami

~

Where there is no love, put love and you will find love.

~

Love in your heart wasn't put there to stay.
Love isn't love 'til you give it away.

~

We may give without loving,
but we cannot love without giving.

~

True love is like flowing water,
it seeks to fill and cover every depth.

-Eduard Woermann

Love wants nothing from your neighbor,
it wants everything for your neighbor.
-Dietrich Bonhoeffer

~

Love is patient, love is kind. It does not envy,
it does not boast, it is not proud. It is not rude,
it is not self-seeking, it is not easily angered,
it keeps no record of wrongs. Love does not
delight in evil but rejoices with the truth.
It always protects, always trusts, always hopes,
always perseveres.
-1 Corinthians 13: 4-7

~

And the story of love is not important - what is important
is that one is capable of love. It is perhaps the only
glimpse we are permitted of eternity.
-Helen Hayes

~

Whoever loves becomes humble.
-Sigmund Freud

~

Where love fails, reason falters.

~

Love gives itself; it is not bought.
-Henry Wadsworth Longfellow

Challenges

Fears are educated into us and can, if we wish,
be educated out.
-Karl Menninger

~

You can measure the size of a man
by the size of the thing that makes him mad.

~

A kiss on the nose does much to turn aside anger.

~

An angry response is better put off until tomorrow.

~

Hatred is like an acid. It can do more damage to the vessel
in which it is stored than to the object on which it is
poured.

~

Smiles are free and easy to give.

~

To sin by remaining quiet when protest is called for
makes men cowards.
-A. Lincoln

Logic cannot overcome a vice.

~

Impatience of the heart melts in the face of love's claim.

~

It is difficult to find the golden mean:
to harden the heart for life, yet
to keep it soft for love.

~

Expectation is a chain connecting all joys.
-Vanvenarguas

~

We will never overcome sadness if we constantly check
our pulse.
-Martin Luther

~

Nothing will content him who is not content with a little.
-Greek proverb

~

Be thine own palace, or the world's thy jail.
-John Donne

~

Patience is power; with time and patience the mulberry
leaf becomes silk.
-Chinese proverb

Where the heart is willing it will find a thousand ways,
but where it is unwilling it will find a thousand excuses.
                                        -*Dayak proverb (Borneo)*

~

Joy

A kind word warms for three winters.
                                        -*Chinese proverb*

~

Cheerfulness is the mother of all virtues.
                                        -*Goethe*

~

What clings to the earth cannot produce a song,
only what rises out of the dust can sing.
                                        -*W. Eigenbrodt*

~

Cheerfulness of the senses makes us happiest.
This quality rewards itself instantly.
                                        -*Schopenhauer*

~

A joke, a laughing word often decide great matters better
and more appropriately than seriousness and sharpness.
                                        -*Horace*

Most folks are about as happy as they make up their minds to be.
              -A. Lincoln

~

To rejoyce easily and often is the mark of noblemindedness.
              -J. Holl

~

And if the heart has a hundred doors,
admit joy through each one of them.
              -Karl Weber

~

Joy, of flame celestial fashioned,
    Daughter of Elysium,
By that holy fire impassioned
    To thy sanctuary we come.
Thine the spells that reunited
    Those estranged by Custom dread,
Every man a brother plighted
    Where thy gentle wings are spread.
      Millions in our arms we gather,
        To the world our kiss be sent!
      Past the starry firmament,
      Brothers, dwells a loving Father.
              -Schiller

~

Cheerful people are not only happy, but generally also good people.
              -K. J. Weber

Life's greatest joys come not from without,
but from the awareness of our own worth
and our value to others.
-v. Bluethgen

~

The true joy of life and the greatest consolation on earth
lie in the disappearance of every opposition to that which
is godly.
-Hilty

~

It is not what we experience, but rather how we perceive
what we experience that determines our destiny.
-Marie v. Ebner-Eschenbach

~

The graces prefer being where there is joy.
-J. Hammer

~

The condition of the body is largely dependent on the soul.
Seek first to be cheerful and calm!
-Wilhelm v. Humboldt

~

To be useful, to bring happiness to those around me,
clears the darkest day and fulfills with quiet delight.
-v. Salis

To earn one's happiness is better than to be resigned
to pain.
-Andre Cide

~

Life without happiness is like the universe without a sun.

~

Not only does joy make happy,
it also paints beauty into the face.

~

Happiness

Happiness lies within us, not with things external.
-K. J. Weber

~

A clean yesterday yields a strong today, and a tomorrow
that is happy and hopeful.
-Goethe

~

If heaven is not within us, we'll search in vain
throughout the universe.
-Otto Ludwig

~

Blessed is he whose echo of golden days gone by
bursts forth comfort for the present.
-Schiller

Rejuvenation is not yours, lest it spring from your soul.
-Goethe

~

Most hope to foster their own happiness by satisfying every wish. Beware of fulfilled dreams where there is no thirst to quench, no task to conquer!
-Montegazza

~

It is in vain for happiness to favor you, unless you realize how very lucky you are.
-Tscherning

~

Why search ever farther? The good lies so near at hand! Just learn to embrace your happiness - it is always there.
-Goethe

~

To shape your happiness ..... worthy fame!
To master your happiness ..... heroe's claim!
-Franz von Schoenthan

~

It is not how your lot in life unfolds, but how you handle it that determines your happiness.
-A. Fromm

~

Who is happy, can make others happy;
who does so, multiplies his own happiness.
-Gleim

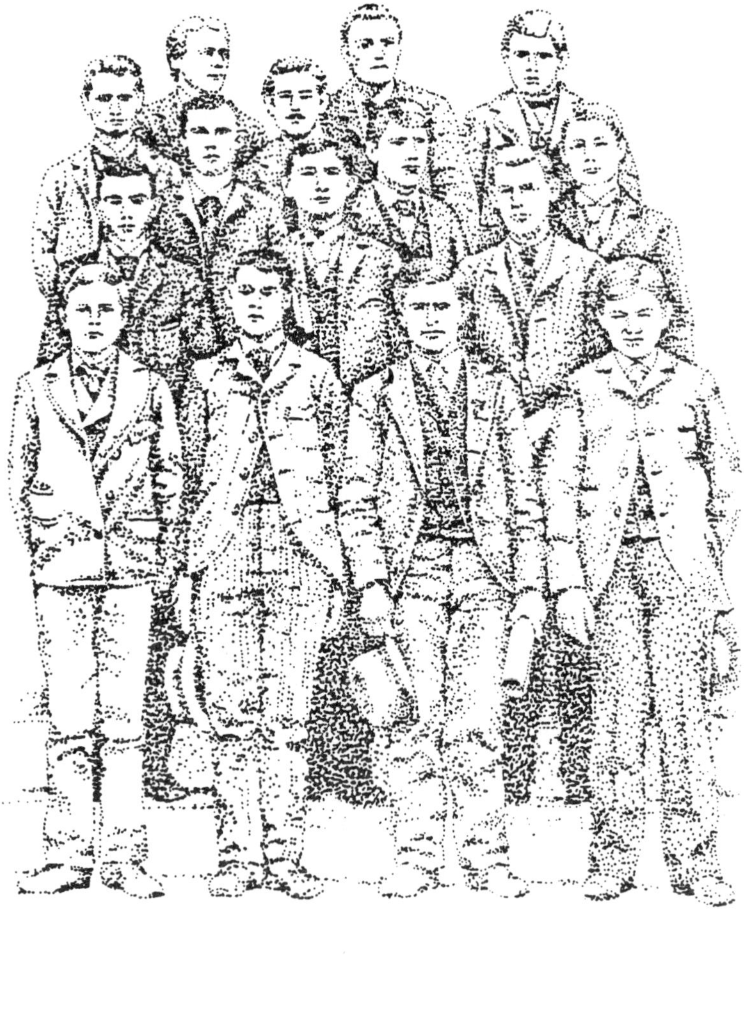

5. The Business of Life

Learning and Teaching

Motivation

Goal Setting

Work

Learning and Teaching

The farther back you can look,
the farther forward you are likely to see.
-*Winston Churchill*

~

I will study and prepare myself so that when my time comes,
I will be ready.
-*A. Lincoln*

~

Language is not just words, but it carries spirit and soul:
through it the sentiment of the people blooms and blooms.
-*Karl Cajka*

~

That which was, nourishes what is to be.
-*F. M. Kuhlmann*

~

The greater the ignorance, the greater the dogmatism.
-*Sir Wm. Osler*

~

The real use of all knowledge is this: that we should dedicate
that reason which was given us by God for the use and
advantage of man.
-*Bacon*

Wise men talk because they have something to say;
fools, because they have to say something.
-Plato

~

There is no knowledge that is not power.

~

The pathway to knowledge is amazing.

~

He who does not read has no advantage over him who
cannot read.
-Robert L. Simpson

~

You can't lead anyone else farther than you've gone yourself.

~

You give but little when you give of your possessions.
It is when you give of yourself that you truly give.
-Kahlil Gibran

~

The true art of memory is the art of attention.
-Samuel Johnson

Let not many of you become teachers, for you know that
we who teach shall be judged with greater strictness.
-James 3:1

~

A teacher affects eternity;
he can never tell where his influence stops.
-Henry Adams

~

The heart of teaching is how teachers feel about their
students.
-Margaret Gullette

~

Learning is becoming, teaching is being.
-Harold Johnson

~

Teaching itself does not make much difference,
however, teachers do.
-McGee

~

Teaching rewards, and rewarding teaches.

~

Go...and teach all nations...teaching them to observe
all the things I have commanded you.
-Matthew 28:19,20

Motivation

The first thought in the morning and the last thought at night are marked on your face and the set of your shoulders.

~

Change your thoughts and you change your world.
                                           -Norman Vincent Peale

~

I can alter my life by altering my attitude of mind.

~

If thou canst believe, all things are possible to him that believeth.
                                           -Mark 9:23

~

A man can have no greater incentive, no greater hope, no greater strength than to know his mother, his sweetheart, or his wife has confidence in him and loves him.
                                           -N. Eldon Tanner

~

The quickest way to acquire self confidence is to do exactly what you are afraid to do.

Courage is grace under pressure.
-Ernest Hemingway

~

Courage is fear holding on another minute.
-G. C. Patton

~

Courage lost - everything's lost.

~

Unpleasantnesses are pills to be swallowed - not chewed.
-Georg Lichtenberg

~

If you wait for perfect conditions,
you will never get anything done.
-Ecclesiastes 11:4

~

Defeat is for those who acknowledge it.

~

It is difficulties that show what men are.
-Epicketus

~

Those things that hurt, instruct.
-B. Franklin

Some see stumbling blocks, others stepping stones.

~

We can complain that the rosebush has thorns,
or we can rejoice that the thornbush has roses.

~

We glory in tribulations also, knowing that tribulation
worketh patience; and patience experience,
and experience hope.
-Romans 5:3,4

~

Take a music bath once or twice a week for a few seasons,
and you will find that it is to the soul what the water bath
is to the body.
-Oliver Wendell Holmes

~

No one knows what he is capable of, lest he try.

~

Either I will find a way, or I will make one.

~

Worse than the quitter is the person who is afraid to begin.

~

If it is to be, it is up to me.

Pray not for lighter loads, but for stronger shoulders.
                                                    -*Elis Gulin*

~

Ask and it shall be given you, seek and ye shall find, knock and it shall be opened onto you.
                                                    -*Matthew 7:7*

~

The present is the only time we truly own; we are expected to use it according to God's will.
                                                    -*Blaise Pascal*

~

You cannot escape the responsibility of tomorrow by evading it today.
                                                    -*A. Lincoln*

~

There is nothing so fatal to character as having finished tasks.

~

Progress is not achieved by the contented.

~

Be not one of those who rather than risk failure, never attempt anything.

~

Footprints in the sands of time are not made by sitting down.

Saints are sinners who keep on trying.

~

It is never too late to be what you might have been.
-George Eliot

Goal Setting

Cherish your visions and your dreams as they are the children of your soul; the blueprints of your ultimate achievements.
-Napoleon Hill

~

Keep true to the dreams of thy youth.

~

Some men see things as they are and say: 'why?';
I dream of things that never were and say: 'why not?'
-Robert Frost

~

Make no little plans; they have no magic to stir men's blood and probably themselves will not be realized. Make big plans, aim high in hope and work, remembering that noble, logical diagram once recorded will never die, but long after we are gone will be a living thing, asserting itself with evergrowing insistency.
-Daniel H. Burnham

~

Not having a goal is more to be feared than not reaching a goal.
-Robert Schuller

~

More people fail through lack of purpose than lack of talent.

Plan your work, then work your plan.

~

Even the longest trip begins with the first step.
-Lao-Tsze

~

Quitters never win. Winners never quit.
-Virginia Hutchinson

~

You can be anything you want to be,
provided you help others to be what they want to be.
-Wong

~

Be what you wish others to become.

~

The only real mistake is the one from which we learn nothing.

~

Experience is a wonderful thing. It enables you to recognize a mistake when you make it again.

~

Past experience should be a guide post, not a hitching post.

Work

Do not pray for tasks equal to your powers.
Pray for powers equal to your tasks.
-Phillips Brooks

~

Think like a man of action; act like a man of thought.
-Henri Bergson

~

Work is love made visible.
-Kahlil Gibran

~

The inner worth of a job cannot be measured in numbers.
-Fritz von Bodelschwing

~

You can easily recognize the truly busy people:
they have time.
-Jules Romain

~

Poems become crystals under high pressure.

~

Ideas don't work, unless we do.

The elimination of weeds, like misunderstandings,
does not tolerate procrastination.
 -Kyrilla Spienka

~

Work done with anxiety about results is far inferior to work
done without anxiety.
 -Bhagavad Gita

~

He labors vainly who endeavors to please every person.
 -Latin Proverb

~

There are two ways to get to the top of a tall oak:
one is to climb it, and the other is to sit on an acorn.

~

Death to the first;
Want to the second;
Bread to the third.

~

Far and away the best prize that life offers is the chance to
work hard at work worth doing.
 -Theodore Roosevelt

~

It hinders the creative work of the mind if the intellect
examines too closely the ideas as they pour in.
 -Friedrich von Schiller

He has half the deed done, who has made a beginning.
                                                                                    -Horace

~

If we all did the things we are capable of doing, we would literally astound ourselves.
                                                                      -Thomas Edison

~

Every task is a self-portrait of the one who does it.

~

If we work upon marble, it will perish;
if we work upon brass, time will efface it...
but if we work upon immortal minds, we engrave on those tablets something which will brighten all eternity.
                                                                     -Daniel Webster

~

Success

Success is going from failure to failure without loss of enthusiasm.
                                                                  -Sir Winston Churchill

~

A winner is a loser who did not quit.

~

Anyone can start, only the best finish.

Success comes before work only in the dictionary.

~

Time stays long enough for anyone who will use it.

~

He is not free who does what he pleases,
but only he who becomes what he should.
-Paul de Lagarde

~

The fool with all his other thoughts, has this also:
he is always getting ready to live.
-Epicurus

~

All you have will someday be given; therefore give now,
that the season of giving may be yours and not your
inheritors'.
-Kahlil Gibran

~

Freedom from desire leads to inner peace.
-Chinese proverb

~

A good name is rather to be chosen than great riches.
-Proverbs 22:1

~

He that walketh with wise men shall be wise.
-Proverbs 13:20

Be determined and confident, for you will be the leader...
Just be determined, be confident...and you will succeed
wherever you go...Study the book of the Law day and
night, and make sure that you obey everything written
in it. Then you will be prosperous and successful.

-Joshua 1:6-8

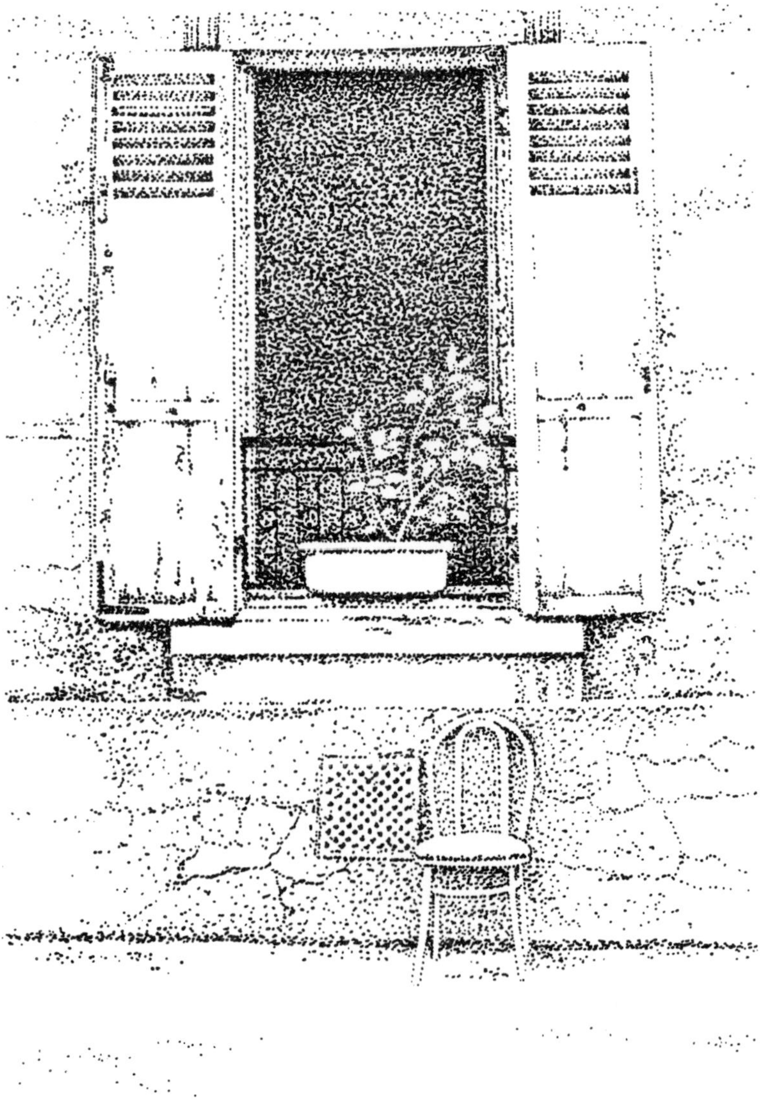

6. The Serene Life

Patience

Peace

Fulfillment

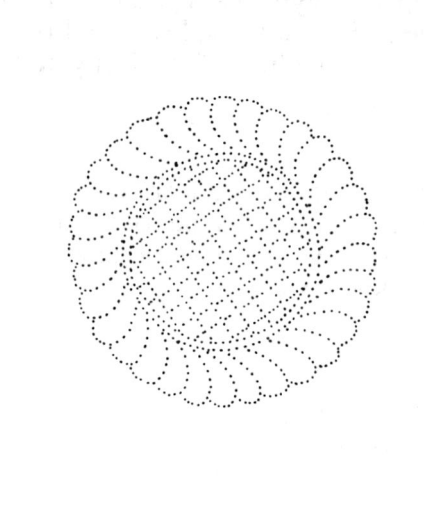

Lord, some day I'll stand before the cliff. I don't want to think about it. What should I do? Some happenings make me think deeply. Maybe that's good, for then I think about you. You live and I know you love me. Lord, <u>is not love life?</u> Well, then there is no cliff: Christ is my life!

~

Waiting is the key to God's understanding. Waiting gives hope its strength. To wait is the fountain of finding. He who has learned to wait, receives a quiet heart. And to have faith means to know waiting.

~

Retain the light of my eyes;
retain the light of my mind;
retain the light of my faith.

-an old man

~

Let me not tire, 'ere I reach the goal. Through your grace lighten my burden. And when my walk begins its last hour, then, o Lord, give your hand to your child.

~

All things are his who knows how to wait.

~

We don't live our sufferings, but inspite of them.

Praises of Thanks from an Older Person

Blessed are those who understand my unsure footing,
    and my lame, shaking hand;
Blessed are those who understand that my ear must strain
    to hear what is being said.
Blessed are those who understand that my eyes are dim,
    and my thoughts are slow;
Blessed are those who give a friendly smile
    and talk with me just a little while.
Blessed are those who don't say: "That story you have told
    me twice already."
Blessed are those who rekindle memories within me.
Blessed are those who let me know that I am being loved,
    honored, and am not left alone.
Blessed are those who through kindness lighten my days,
    and look with me down the road
    to the home eternal.

~

For the unlearned, old age is winter,
for the learned, it is the season of harvest.
-Hasidic saying

~

It is with life as with a play: what matters is not how long it is, but how good it is.
-Seneca

~

He who has a 'why' to live can bear most any 'how.'
-Friedrich Nietzsche

For God so loved the world that he gave his one and only Son, that whoever believes in him shall not perish but have eternal life.
-John 3:16

~

You know the depth of a man's soul by studying the motions of his face.
-Dimitri Mitropolous

~

...no one can change into defeat the victory of one who has vanquished himself.
-Buddha

~

Quiet minds cannot be perplexed or frightened, but go on in fortune or misfortune at their own private pace, like a clock in a thunder storm.
-Robert Louis Stevenson

~

The holiest of all holidays are those kept by ourselves in silence and apart; the secret anniversaries of the heart.
-Henry Wadsworth Longfellow

~

Great joys, like griefs, are silent.
-Shackerly Marmion

Calmness is not exhausted waiting, but an inner alertness.
-H. Huemmer

~

The greatest events are not our loudest,
but the quietest hours.
-Nietzsche

~

Justice and the blood of Christ,
these are my dress and ornaments
with these before God I will plead
when into heaven I shall go.

David and Anna surrounded by some of their loved ones.